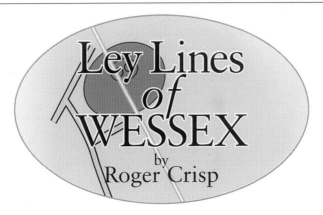

Ley Lines of WESSEX
by Roger Crisp

Contents

The lay and lie of the land

Below:

Old Sarum and Salisbury Cathedral (centre) which are on the same ley line.

At a local level you will see, if you open an Ordnance Survey map, that the tallest cathedral spire in England appears on the same line as Clearbury Ring, the massive earthwork hill fort of Old Sarum and, further north, one of the most important ancient sites in the world, Stonehenge. Ancient burial mounds, tumuli, are on the line further north.

If there are alignments further north, what about further south? Yes, the line continues, near an ancient burial chamber called The Giant's Long Barrow near Castle Hill, until it brushes the edge of another earthwork similar to Clearbury Ring, called Frankenbury Camp.

You may now want to investigate 'ley lines' further.

The line you have just followed was a line you could not actually see on the ground. You would see features that *suggested* a line. This line, or alignment, is an example of what have become called 'ley lines'. Here you have re-lived the experience of the founder of ley line theory, Alfred Watkins. His reaction to a similar experience, whilst travelling on horseback in his native Herefordshire

as one of sheer excitement. He felt as if he had had a revelation, an insight into knowledge now largely lost to modern mankind. He was sure that the alignment he had seen was not a coincidence.

Watkins, though, was no New Age traveller, nor a fanciful man. As a serious businessman, inventor and natural scientist, he set about proving or disproving his theory. He firmly believed that the alignment, and others, had been planned. For him they were routes, old paths, ancient roads, or 'old straight tracks'.

Below:
Woodhenge, Durrington.

Whether ley lines exist or not is still very hotly debated. This small book hopes to give you a clear introduction to the ideas involved. It will also give you a good reason to wander, and wonder, around the glorious Wessex countryside. Whether or not you finally dismiss the theory of ley lines, you will certainly enjoy the investigation. Unfamiliar and odd, out of the way spots, as well as the famous areas, will have a new and renewed interest for you. Enjoy the journey.

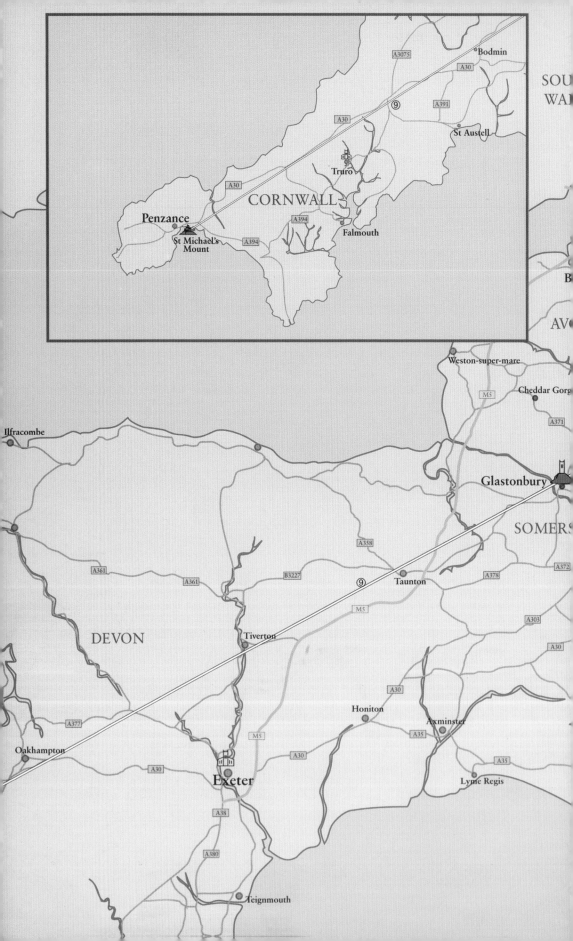

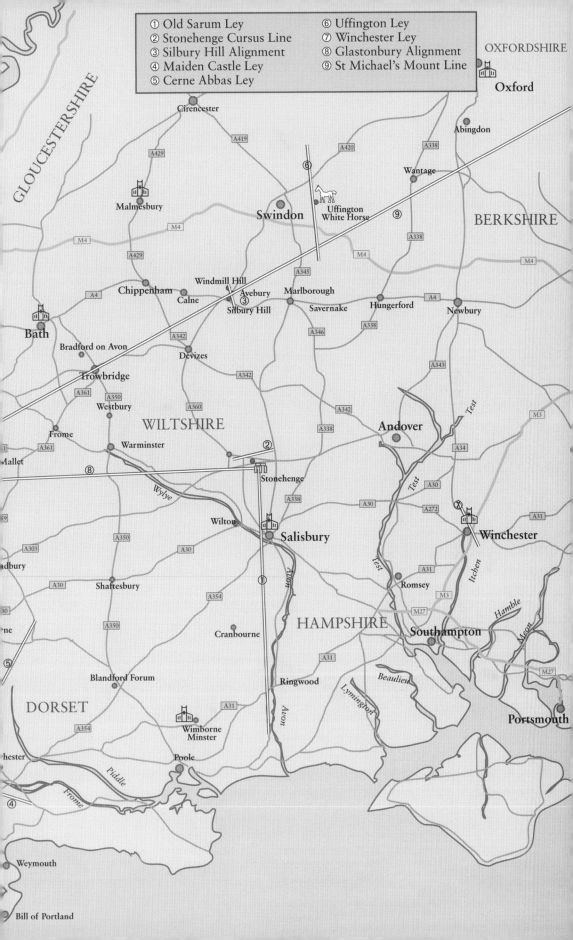

① Old Sarum Ley
② Stonehenge Cursus Line
③ Silbury Hill Alignment
④ Maiden Castle Ley
⑤ Cerne Abbas Ley
⑥ Uffington Ley
⑦ Winchester Ley
⑧ Glastonbury Alignment
⑨ St Michael's Mount Line

OXFORDSHIRE

Oxford

GLOUCESTERSHIRE

Cirencester

A419

A429

Malmesbury

A420

A338

Abingdon

Wantage

⑥

Uffington
White Horse

⑨

BERKSHIRE

Swindon

M4

M4

A345

A338

M4

A4

A429

Chippenham

Calne

Windmill Hill

③

Avebury

Silbury Hill

Marlborough

Savernake

Hungerford

A4

Newbury

Bath

Bradford on Avon

A342

A346

A338

Trowbridge

Devizes

A342

A343

A361

A350

Westbury

A342

Frome

A360

WILTSHIRE

A338

Test

M3

A303

A361

Mallet

Warminster

⑧

Wylye

②

Stonehenge

A338

Andover

A34

Test

A30

A272

⑦

A31

Winchester

Wilton

A350

A30

A30

Itchen

Romsey

Salisbury

①

Avon

A31

M3

Shaftesbury

A30

A354

Beaulieu

Hamble

Meon

Southampton

M27

A350

Cranbourne

HAMPSHIRE

A31

Blandford Forum

Ringwood

DORSET

A31

Avon

Lymington

Portsmouth

A354

Wimborne
Minster

⑤

Poole

Piddle

chester

Frome

④

Weymouth

Bill of Portland

It is impossible to introduce the subject of ley lines without reference to the Herefordshire businessman Alfred Watkins, born in 1855. He was employed by his father as a brewer's travelling representative. From travelling on horseback he became very well acquainted with the landscape and its features. Fortunately, he was a keen, early photographer, inventor (pinhole camera, Watkins

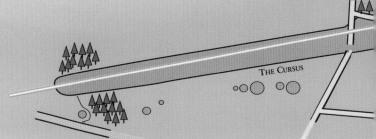

THE CURSUS

**STONEHENGE
CURSUS LINE**

exposure meter) naturalist and amateur archaeologist, who kept copious notes.

However, it wasn't until the age of 65 that the 'revelation' of ley lines struck him. He suddenly noticed that certain features of the landscape appeared to be standing along exactly straight lines and intersected traditionally sacred places. He himself recalled that the 'ley system came in a flash of insight like a system of glowing wires.

He never took anything as self evident and put his 'insight' to the test. Working back over his keen local knowledge he sought out more examples of features on straight lines. With his camera he set about making a record of his experiences. This was published in 1925 as *The Old Straight Track*. It is still the most relevant book to read and has been republished, as has his second, slimmer volume, *The Ley Hunter's Guide*.

Watkins was convinced that he had rediscovered some long since forgotten knowledge of our most remote ancestors. In his prefaces he talks of the 'Discovery, or "Rediscovery" of the "Spirit of the British Countryside"'. He realized that such places as mounds, single standing stones, mark stones and holy water wells occurred on the lines he was following, so he drew up a sort of check list of possible features that might indicate a ley line.

Places joined by straight lines, what could be simpler? Surely you can join any random points with straight lines? Probably true, but what struck Watkins was that the sites that *he* kept joining together did *not* appear to be random points. Stonehenge, for example, is hardly a random point, whatever the explanation favoured for its existence. People do not drag huge rocks tens,

MY MAIN THEME IS THE ALIGNMENT ACROSS MILES OF COUNTRY OF A GREAT NUMBER OF OBJECTS, OR SITES OF OBJECTS, OF PREHISTORIC ANTIQUITY.

Alfred Watkins

To Durrington

Woodhenge

Cuckoo Stone

Long Barrow (not evident)

N

The Cursus

Old King Barrows

New King Barrows

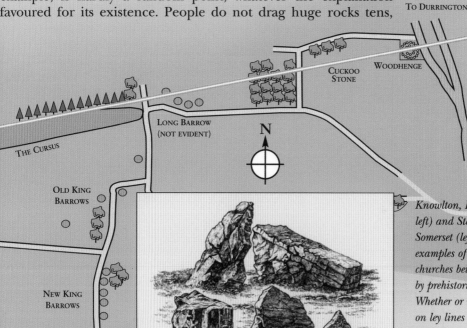

Knowlton, Dorset (far left) and Stanton Drew, Somerset (left) are notable examples of Christian churches being built in or by prehistoric sites. Whether or not they are on ley lines is a different matter; Stanton Drew may stand at the end of two lines. One goes through Glastonbury Tor to Dundon Hill Fort, and the other through various tumuli and a church, to Henton Church.

even hundreds of miles over 3000 years just for the fun of it. It would be strange for a civilization to spend thousands of man hours digging ditches and earthworks on the massive scale of Maiden Castle or Avebury because there was nothing better to do.

Ley Lines in Perspective

Below:
Glastonbury and the Tor.

First of all, let's clear up the word *ley* itself. It is an old Anglo-Saxon word meaning an enclosed field. But it appears to have an older meaning referring to a simple clearing, pasture or glade. As the word *leye* it seems also to have an obsolete, but for our purposes, interesting meaning of 'flame' or 'fire', as well as 'island'. Its root is also found in the word 'lake' and, with it, means 'reflection'. All these elements – clearings, water, fire – are relevant to us as we shall see.

The word is still found as part of village and town names today in several forms: *lay, lei, ley, leigh, lea, lee.* Watkins combined the ideas associated with the word in using it for his lines. In the heavily wooded Anglo-Saxon and earlier landscape of Wessex, seeing a mile or several miles ahead would depend upon clearings and glades to allow lines of sight for direction, perhaps to see the sun, stars, moon or fires built as beacons and markers.

Trackways would necessarily find their way to and from these clearings. Thus a track or path would also be associated with the word *ley*. Watkins suggests that the main commodity carried on the track could give it its name, such as Whitley (salt) and Fishley. Thus *ley* would easily come to mean a track or route as opposed to 'field'. Fish and salt do not grow in fields. The shortest path between two points is always a straight line. Hence the title of Watkins' first book, *The Old Straight Track*.

GLASTONBURY
ALIGNMENT

STEP ONE: looking at a map.

Watkins identified the following features as clues to detecting a ley line. Initially using a good ordnance, he suggests searching for the following. Mark them with a highlighter pen. Once you've finished you can step back and see how rich the area you have chosen is in potential features for joining together with straight ley lines.

- Ancient Mounds are found under a bewildering array of old language and dialect names (BARROW, BURG, BURGH, BURY, BUTT, CAIRN, CASTLE, CRUC, GARN, HOW, KNAPP, KNOWL, LOW, MARY, MOAT, MOOT, MOUND, MOUNT, TOOT, TUMP, TUMULUS, TWT). Some of these words have also taken on different meanings, so we must be careful with BURGH, BURY, CASTLE AND KNOWL, for example.
- Ancient stones (not the ones marked 'boundary stone', which are probably too recent in origin).
- Moats, islands in lakes, small lakes, ponds.
- Traditional or 'holy' wells.
- Beacon points, and other dwellings, farms with the same name.
- Crossroads with place names given them, ancient wayside crosses.
- Churches, hermitages, cathedrals, abbeys of ancient foundation.
- Ancient castles, and old 'castle' place names – remember the name CAMP has been, over the years, interchangeable with CASTLE.

To see what I mean, take Ordnance Survey Map number 184 of the Landranger series, for 'Salisbury and The Plain'. Then, highlight every barrow, long barrow, tumulus, group of tumuli, earthwork, ditch, dyke, camp, castle, ring, circle, mizmaze and major ancient sites. You will find your map is covered with ancient and less ancient sites.

STEP TWO

Having marked these features clearly, take a certain marker point (say a mound or ancient stone) pin a straight edge ruler or a taut piece of cotton to it. Then slowly rotate the cotton in a circle, covering as much of the map as possible. Keep your eyes focussed on whether other features you've highlighted seem to appear on a straight line along the tight cotton thread. You may possibly have found a ley line, but there is more checking to do.

STEP THREE

Allowing for a little inaccuracy in your measuring for now, but not in your final conclusion, can you find four features on your line? This was Watkins' minimum number which he felt meant that the alignment was probably not just a coincidence. Only three points could always be a coincidence, but if you have found three it may be worth looking more carefully, either within the area already identified or by extending the line into an adjacent map area. Now look more closely along the line. Are there any features, no matter how far away, that appear to be on the line? Do any stretches of old roads follow the line at any time? If so, then it is increasingly likely that you may have found a ley line.

STEP FOUR: Getting out and about.

Now it is time for fresh air. Time to try and walk along the line you have identified to see if it looks feasible. Maybe other pieces of evidence will turn up that were not obvious on the map. Perhaps the line will cross a river at an old ferry or ford point. Fixed observation points may present themselves to you, such as a church, mound or ancient ring earthwork, on a distant bank that keeps recurring in the same line of sight as you travel. Watkins was amazed at how often a ley line crossed a modern road through field gates on either side. Remember that, out in the landscape itself, you must be a detective rather than a surveyor.

St Laurence's Church, Holwell

Dungeon Hill Fort

Holy Well

Abbey Remains

Cerne Abbas Ley

N

Cerne Abbas Giant

Smecan Down Longbarrow

Below:
Cerne Abbas Giant.

Tumuli

Cross Dyke

Grimstone Down Tumuli

Long Barrow

Tumuli

Winterborne Steepleton Church

Bonkham Hill Tumuli

Whaddon Tumulus

Objections & Queries

**Why should
Burial Mounds
be linked to
anything else?**

Perhaps ley lines are simply 'bats' in the imaginations of Watkins and others. Watkins was aware of those who thought his ideas ridiculous. Many still do today. Their main objections are surely worthy of consideration.

Hundreds of burial mounds can be found in South Wiltshire and Dorset; surely it proves nothing that many are aligned. In fact it seems inevitable. Thus they would not be necessary as sighting points for ley lines.

An answer is that the original sites of the first mounds, which may well have been important for ley lines, took over in importance as sacred places as ley line trackways fell into increasing disuse. If the leys were tracks, then they certainly have become obso-

lete and this process must have started a long time ago. After all, our church graveyards do not mean that the church itself was built for the dead.

How can the pre-Christian site of, say, an ancient earthwork be significantly linked with, say, the site of a church or cathedral built 3000 or 4000 years later? On what basis can the sites figure in Watkins' 'old straight tracks'?

The starting point for the answer would be that in a landscape like Wessex, that has seen so many races and civilizations come and go, what appears at first to be a modern site may actually have underlying roots that stretch back hundreds, if not thousands, of years. A striking example would be the church and whole village in the middle of the huge Avebury circle.

Mediaeval churches, moats and castles indicating prehistoric trackways?

Maiden Castle, Dorset, is a vast marvel of prehistoric engineering used variously by Iron Age warriors and Roman soldiers. The Maiden Castle ley runs along one edge of it (see p.4).

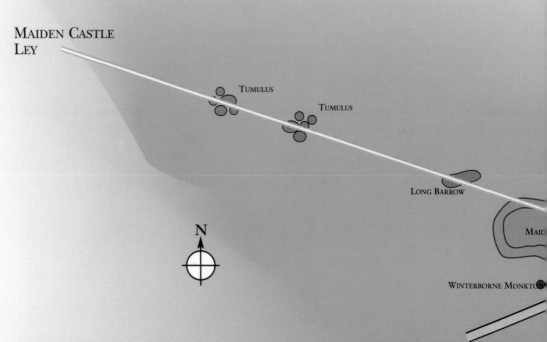

MAIDEN CASTLE
LEY

TUMULUS

TUMULUS

LONG BARROW

N

MAID

WINTERBORNE MONKTO

**Prehistoric
Britain was
covered in thick
forests, so how
could there have
been long, sight
line trackways?**

If the ley lines represent paths and routes surely it would have
been impossible to make them since woods and forests were so
dense any sighting points would be obscured. That would have
forced the people using any tracks to go up onto the high ridges,
if they were above the forests.

Early road users, and therefore their roads, would just have gone
the easy way, which does not necessarily mean in straight lines.

The great highways such as the Fosse Way, Watling Street,
Ermine Street, may be pre-Roman. If they are not, and were only
built in Roman times, the landscape was just as densely wooded on
their arrival and yet the Romans built roads which still exist and
are in use today. Why could earlier Britons not have done so?

The idea that prehistoric man could have laid out, or even
wanted to lay out, such precise alignments on the landscape was
regarded as impossible in Watkins' time. Those early occupants of
human history were seen as ignorant, ape-like at best, and mathe-
matically backward. However, with our research into the history of
5000 years ago, we know that the builders of Stonehenge and
Avebury in Wessex were far from primitive, banana chomping
chimps. What's more Julius Caesar, on reaching Britain in 54BC,
noted in his journals how the priest class of the early Britons stud-
ied advanced mathematics and astronomy.

Such an advanced people and their predecessors may easily have followed the same instinct of sighting a route from a hill top, and marking its way with stones, mounds and natural notches in the horizon. The more we learn of early humans everywhere, the more we find that there was probably a lot more communication and trade between distant tribes and incoming invaders than we have previously given them credit for.

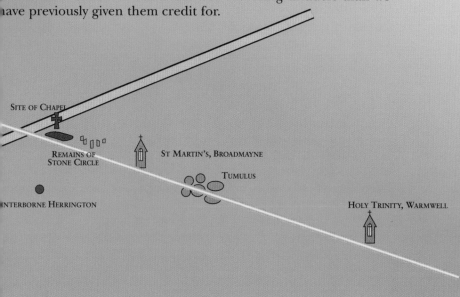

SITE OF CHAPEL

REMAINS OF STONE CIRCLE

ST MARTIN'S, BROADMAYNE

TUMULUS

WINTERBORNE HERRINGTON

HOLY TRINITY, WARMWELL

Beyond Watkins

Earth Energy lines

Watkins' initial ideas related to tracks and pathways have since been taken further. His ideas of straight lines over the landscape have echoes around many civilisations ancient and modern.

These are akin to the body's acupuncture lines of Chinese medicine. Needle points in Chinese acupuncture and acupressure are where energy flows in the body can be regulated, reversed and the body treated for cures. Similarly, in the Chinese 'science' of 'Feng Shui', the same principles apply to the body of the Earth. Temples and sacred places are built on the 'needle' points of the earth and the ceremonies and rituals that take place there are helping to regulate and 'cure' the energy flow in the Earth.

Dowsing

Dowsing is regarded by many people as a way of 'feeling' and 'finding' energy, water, minerals, lost objects by a person – the dowser – who is especially sensitive. Some dowsers use physical instruments like forked branches of hazel wood, or metal 'L' shaped rods, or pendulums which will move, twitch or in some physical way respond to unseen energy sources. Many of these people are sure that 'ley line energy', and also 'sacred site energy' can be detected by these methods. The sacred sites, and many of those features described by Watkins as features on a ley line, are similar to the 'needle' points mentioned above.

Is there any way of sensing 'ley lines', as opposed to looking on maps and the ground for alignments? Dowsing is the practice of searching 'blind' for something by holding metal rods, forked hazel twigs or pendulums. When the object being sought is nearby these instruments will respond – jerk, rotate or swing – in the hands of the dowser. Different dowsers use different grips, some are specialized in searching for particular things. Water dowsing is the most widely known practice. However, underground electric power cables, mineral ores, lost objects, even lost people are on record as having been found by dowsing.

Ralph Whitlock, a revered natural historian, country affairs writer and renowned dowser, cites the work of the archaeologist Guy Underwood, who became increasingly sure that ancient megalithic sites, and especially standing stones, were purposely built over 'blind springs', as he called them, or underground water sources. Underwood goes on to say that it is unfortunate that dowsing has been connected only with water. He adds that this may be a fragment of a much larger picture representing 'the existence of a geophysical force so far not identified'. He refers to the force as representing 'geodetic lines'.

Underwood also feels that dowsers are not so much responding to water, which is everywhere underground, but to the underground fissures through which it is passing under varied pressure.

He identified two types of dowser. The 'negative dowser', a kind of generalised version, feels a response in the rough vicinity of a blind spring. The 'positive dowser', the rarer of the two, will get a very strong reaction, but only when directly over the source. These are the people who can detect the various lines.

According to Underwood there are three kinds of dowsing lines, the third of which are called 'tracklines ... because on the surface they were usually marked by the course of some ancient track or field boundary'.

Background picture:
Feint image of Avebury stones, which responde to dowsing.

Below:
Ralph Whitlock demonstrating dowsing.

The conventional forked twig of the dowser is, in effect, simply the counterpart of the pointer on a spring-balance and has no intrinsic merit. The two arms of the fork are convenient because one can be held by each hand, but some dowsers operate efficiently with a straight wand. I am often asked, 'Is it necessary for the twig to be of hazel?' No, it is not. I have used elm, willow and a number of exotic woods overseas. The only criterion is that they must be reasonably fibrous and flexible and so able to stand stress without snapping. I doubt the statement that the ancient Druids used apple twigs; apple wood seems far too brittle. It is not even necessary to use wood at all. No doubt the convention arose centuries ago in rural areas where a twig cut from a hedge was the only tool readily available. Baling wire or wire from a coat-hanger is an acceptable substitute. I have often operated with a length of thickish wire, twisted to a convenient shape.

Water Divining & other Dowsing – A Practical Guide,
Ralph Whitlock

Below:
Winchester Cathedral.

Below right:
St Catherine's Hill,
Winchester, from the
water meadows.

Whitlock tells us that the French researchers, M. Merle and M. Diot, working in the 1930s, found that a very large number of standing stones were situated on the intersection of two or more of Underwood's dowsing lines. Two British dowsers – Capt. F.L.M. Boothby and R. Allender Smith – copied the research in Britain and found that the same was true of barrows, sacred stones and more examples of the array of prehistoric features on the landscape.

They referred to 'knots' of converging lines and Smith coined the phrase 'blind springs' later taken up by Underwood. In his notes and books Smith gives these knots more defined shapes and categories: spirals, whorls, 'reversed circles', arcs, and more. Underwood maintained that it was not only well-known Wessex sites situated on these knots (Avebury, Stonehenge, the Cerne Abbas Giant and the Uffington White Horse), but so too were many other megalithic features, big and small, especially tumuli that can be found in such abundance at the heart of Wessex in Wiltshire and Dorset.

The implication is that shapes *in* the ground, as identified by dowsers, are perhaps mirrored as features *on* the ground – rings, concentric circles, spirals. According to the theories of recent thinkers, these underground sites would have been located by the dowsers, diviners and priests of these times. Thus, the sites would represent important sources of earth energy and monuments of whatever sort would then be built.

Underwood was sure in his own mind that these sites, both ancient and more recent, were located on the site of 'blind' springs. He produced detailed diagrams for prehistoric sites of all sizes.

He was also convinced that many features of much more recent origin had the same site credentials. Again this takes in both the large and the small. The massive examples are structures such as the great mediaeval cathedrals of Salisbury and Winchester in Wessex, as well as further afield at Chichester and Westminster Abbey. Underwood drew up detailed plans of all four to illustrate his ideas. The smaller but no less significant are the sites of parts of actual churches such as the altar, chancel, font, stoops and spirit bowls. Beyond churches themselves he also includes gateways, ponds, fords, churchyard walls and even traditional gallows and gibbets – public execution sites. Is this last example perhaps, then, some throwback to the Celtic and pre-Celtic days of human sacrifice?

Above:
St. Catherine's Hill from the south, looking towards the city and cathedral.

WINCHESTER LEY

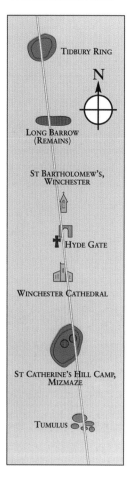

Stones and energy

There are undoubtedly inaccuracies in Underwood's work but that does not obscure his underlying principles. His list of features found on the lines is also the same as those of Alfred Watkins. Both were writing independently and at around the same time as the Frenchmen, Merle and Diot.

That dowsers are responding to *something* seems clear enough. It is, however, *not* clear that all dowsers are reacting to the *same* forces. Some aspect of the earth's electromagnetism may be the cause of shuddering hazel twigs and rotating pendulums. However, water in some form or other still appears to be of importance. After all, water has always been of prime, and primaeval, importance.

One of the most fascinating aspects of dowsing on ley lines, and of the features that appear along them, is the repeated reference by the dowsers to feelings and currents of 'whirling', 'whorls', 'circles', 'spirals', 'knots', 'reversed circles'.

An aerial view of, say, Stonehenge, Avebury, Glastonbury Tor, Maiden Castle, Old Sarum or even of Silbury Hill, shows a pattern of circles, concentric circles or circles within circles. Indeed many of these places have the shape in their name today: Figsbury Rings, north of Salisbury; Clearbury Ring to the south of the town; Badbury Rings near Wimborne Minster; Knowlton Ring, in Dorset, Tidbury Ring, in Hampshire.

That circles are important in folklore, whether or not they occur naturally or have to be built, is evident in the importance attached to stones with holes in them. For example, in Cornwall, the Men-an-Tol near Morvah – also called the Crick Stone – was used for curing rickets. Children were passed through it as a ritual cure. Similar customs are found attached to stones all over the world. Hands have traditionally been passed through smaller holes in a large stone to mark a betrothal or binding promise.

Is the idea of stones, having power, being alive, really so outlandish? The way we think of words is important. No, you don't farm stones, nor feed them, nor talk to them. But, are they really 'without life' in the sense of having no discernible movements within them? What about quartz which can vibrate like a pulse on a micro level? Or granite, such as in Cornwall, which is always giving off radiation? In a sense these are alive. Could there be some sensation that we no longer use which picks up feelings from such stones?

WINDMILL HILL

N

AVEBURY MANOR MUSEUM

Above:
Avebury.

AVEBURY

A4361

TO BECKHAMPTON & A4 ←

WEST KENNET AVENUE

B4003

Below:
Silbury Hill.

SILBURY HILL

SILBURY HILL
ALIGNMENT

A4

A4

TO CALNE & BATH

TO MARLBOROUGH
& LONDON →

WEST KENNETT LONG BARROW

The Evil Eye

Throughout the Middle East and Far East is the concept (and danger) of the Evil Eye. Wherever you find humans you will probably find reference to the Evil Eye. It may stem simply from the sense of being uneasy under another person's gaze or surveillance. That sense of being 'watched' by a 'Big Brother' figure pervaded Orwell's *1984*. It can also be from a sense of being watched by an envious eye which seems to be very much the idea throughout the Mediterranean and the Middle East. Hence the strict warning against covetousness in the religions from this part of the world Judaism, Christianity and Islam.

We shouldn't underestimate the power of this fear of envy from either humans or the Gods. In the Ancient Greek myths it occurs time and again, right from the founding characters of Gaia and Uranus, then on to the next generation with Chronos.

There are references to the Evil Eye idea, it seems, as far back as 3,000 BC in the writings of the Sumerians. Also, in Ancient Egyptian mythology, Horus fought his evil brother Seth. Horus castrated Seth, rendering his evil powerless, but Seth tore out and buried one of Horus's eyes.

The important thing then is to find a means of protection from the Evil Eye, regardless of why it might exist. Again, the Evil Eye sees in straight lines. Apart from wearing an eye of Horus on a brooch, for example, to deflect the Eye, there are many other methods of protection.

Having one good eye is still today a powerful talisman. Look on the prow of traditional fishing boats in Greece and Turkey and you will see them protected by the single eye of Horus.

Straight lines from afar

Japanese Shinto temples show evidence of deliberate straight line sitings. In Chinese geomancy better known to us as feng shui and in many other old shamanistic cultures, the spirits, and evil particularly, are believed to travel only in straight lines. The way to fool the evil spirits therefore is to block their path, deflecting them from access to the key, central or sacred point. A miz-maze on the ground would symbolically do just this. These mazes in Britain have also been called 'Troy Town' or, later, Drayton. It is speculated that this derives from the Celtic 'troi' meaning 'to turn', or from 'tro' meaning 'a flux of time'. One such 'Troy Town' used to exist at Pimperne, in Dorset, up to the middle of the 17th century.

Opposite page
Miz-maze on St. Catherine's Hill, Winchester.

In both the Americas much more mapping and evaluation has been done. In Ohio the Hopewell people of 2000 years ago left massive earthworks and straight road systems. Again these were a combination of real and symbolic tracks. The Miwok, of California

Inset picture
The plan of a labyrinth or 'Troy Town', ploughed up at Pimperne in 1730.

Background:

The mysterious white horse at Uffington is more than 2000 years old. It is on the same ley as the curious flat-topped dragon hill which is thought by some to be where St. George slew the dragon.

the Anaszi of New Mexico, unknown people of Costa Rica and the Mayans of Mexico's Yucatan peninsula created similar systems.

In South America, the Nazca desert lines of Peru have been known to the outside world since 1939, but barely understood. They are suspected to date from at least the 6th century. Whatever their purpose obviously a great deal of work and importance was attached to the necessity for straight lines. But now there are lines and trackways (both symbolic and actual) running in straight lines from other tribes and peoples such as are being researched in Bolivian temple alignments. The Incas and pre-Incas of Peru had massive straight-line road systems stretching over some of the worst possible terrain. Such systems are also reported, though unresearched, in Venezuela.

The Central American Mayan Indian tribes built temples on straight lines. Still today they say that there are two kinds of road between the sites. One is under the surface of the earth. The other is in the air. Both, like our ley lines, are invisible. One of the most important ley line examples in Britain is in Wessex. It is the Salisbury ley which runs over 18 miles from a tumulus to the north of Stonehenge, then southwards through Stonehenge, Old Sarum, Salisbury Cathedral, Clearbury Ring and on to Frankenbury Camp.

UFFINGTON LEY

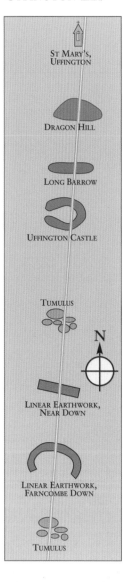

ST MARY'S,
UFFINGTON

DRAGON HILL

LONG BARROW

UFFINGTON CASTLE

TUMULUS

N

LINEAR EARTHWORK,
NEAR DOWN

LINEAR EARTHWORK,
FARNCOMBE DOWN

TUMULUS

Right:
*Salisbury Cathedral was
built to replace Old Sarum
(see page 2); both are on
the same ley line.*

Firstly, the aerial line. The city of Salisbury and a cathedral were originally sited on top of the massive earthwork mound (now to the north of today's city) called Old Sarum. It was decided to move the city off the hilltop in the 12th century. Legend has it that the site of the new cathedral, the kingpin of that new city, was decided by firing an arrow from the top of Old Sarum. Wherever the arrow landed was to be the site of the cathedral.

Today's cathedral is sited on what was originally watery, boggy water meadows. These then had to be drained. Hardly a clever, thought out and reasonable site from an engineering angle. Yet it is directly beside a river – the Avon – which brings in our water connection again, and it is still, as was the former cathedral, on the proposed ley line. A coincidence? If the use of the arrow were symbolic of moving in a straight line that would make more sense. If the ley line were simply a track way, as proposed by Alfred Watkins, then also the new site would have been an important crossing point of the rivers that meet there. Indeed the original old bridge is directly beyond the cathedral close at Harnham. It is part of the original old road that leads, on the same straight line, in the direction of Clearbury Ring.

Secondly, the underground line. Having come across the idea of ley lines almost twenty years ago and having never heard of Clearbury Ring despite being from Salisbury, I decided to go and take a look at it. I had just read Alfred Watkins' book and thought this would be a good test. The ring, being obscured by trees, is hard to make out until you are directly on it. You cannot make the appropriate sight lines to test the view of the ley line. However, as Watkins had noticed at several places before, I found a Scots pine tree. This tree he reckoned is often, incongruously, found like a kind of marker.

Being quite pleased with the experiment I found my way from the ring back down to the road. As I emerged an old man was walking by. He greeted me and asked if I had been up on the ring. I told him I had, a little unsure of myself, wondering if I had been trespassing. With a slightly secretive air he said, 'You know, they do say there's a secret tunnel that runs all the way straight to the Ring from the cathedral down in the town'. This was in 1980.

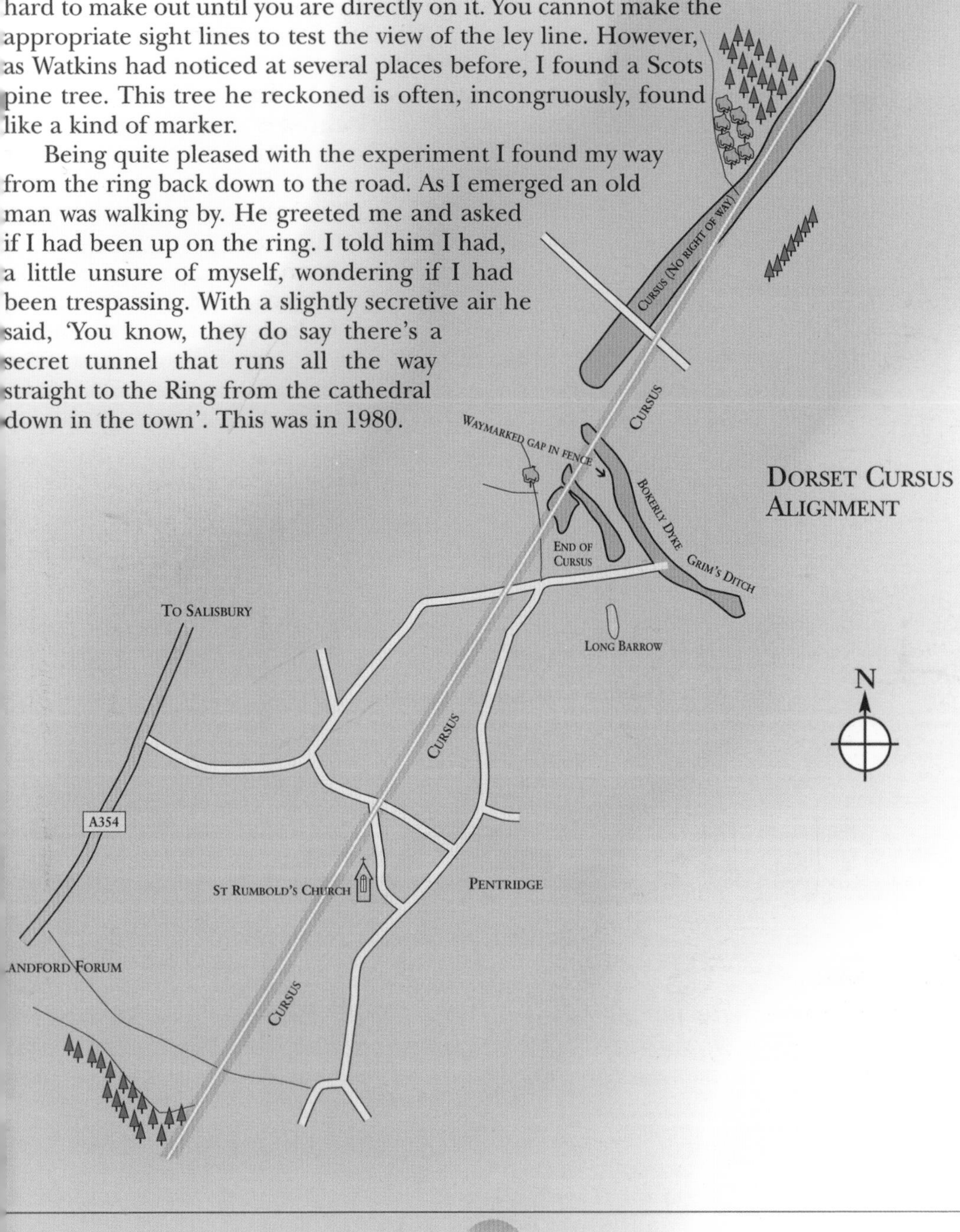

DORSET CURSUS
ALIGNMENT

CURSUS (NO RIGHT OF WAY)

CURSUS

WAYMARKED GAP IN FENCE

BOKERLY DYKE

GRIM'S DITCH

END OF CURSUS

TO SALISBURY

LONG BARROW

N

CURSUS

A354

ST RUMBOLD'S CHURCH

PENTRIDGE

BLANDFORD FORUM

CURSUS

Folklore

IF THE ROOTS OF
ARCHAEOLOGY ARE
BOUND UP WITH
FOLKLORE ... PERHAPS
FOLKLORE CAN HOLD
THE BALANCE
BETWEEN RATIONALISM
AND SYMBOLISM.

Jeremy Harte

Snakes and serpents still hiss down the ages

Watkins regarded folklore as a fundamental source of information. It is the possibility of the symbolic importance of these stories which is critical here.

Memories from societies that haven't developed writing are usually passed on by word of mouth. After writing evolves the oral tradition can quickly vanish. But traces are often left in 'fairy tales' and rhymes, whose meaning becomes increasingly unclear down the generations, although the stories still survive. Sometimes the reason for the story is forgotten or misremembered, though the story still continues. These misrememberings occur in all forms of the language, not just in stories, but also in place names, people's names, slang and festivals.

Many hills and forts have stories of being guarded by a great serpent, a coiled snake, a dragon or a giant worm. This may be a vivid telling of how a circle or concentric circle (physical or invisible such as with our dowsers) was somehow associated with the spot. If you look down on a coiled snake it is exactly that – a spiral, a circle, a series of circles, all at the same time.

One interesting aspect of snakes, serpents, griffins, dragons and worms (taken as generally to represent the same sort of creature) is that their significance has varied throughout the history of our culture. They have not always been reviled and loathed as they mostly are today.

The poetry of Earth is never dead KEATS, 1816

Ages before the Bible they were regarded as guardians of knowledge, and then by association as sentinels over other more tangible objects such as great hordes of treasure. The book of Genesis picked up this significance with the age old, pre-Biblical, story of the 'Tree of Knowledge' and of the Serpent that gave the apple – the fruit of that important tree – to Adam and Eve.

Many of the pagan sacred sites were on hill tops and mounds, presumably because the sun, moon and stars would have been so important in their rituals and beliefs. How many of these mounds have now been overlain with the name of a dragon slayer important to Christianity? St Michael's Mount in Cornwall and St Michael's Church on top of Glastonbury Tor seem to be two good, large examples.

These two sites are also on the proposed, exceptionally long, ley line reaching from South Cornwall (the farthest tip of Outer Wessex), then north-east through Wessex, including Avebury, and on up to the coast of East Anglia. Significantly this line is the one the Midsummer Sunrise traces across southern England. What is more this sun alignment line, and others, are often associated in folklore with serpents and dragons.

Watkins regarded the ley lines as tracks, or physical routes. From our own folklore and other cultures we see the idea of straight lines having a deeper, spiritual significance. If the notion of a network of lines seems feasible in the first place, it would also seem feasible that both explanations are equal parts of the same picture.

Background:
Saint Michael's Mount, Cornwall, a fabled and holy place.

Below:
The Cheesewring, Cornwall, thought by some to be part of the remains of vast interconnected storage temples.

John Michell, in *The View Over Atlantis*, discusses Chinese geo
mancy and fung-shui in relation to ley lines.

A hundred years ago the practice of Chinese geomancy firs
became generally known in the West through the complaints c
European business men, who found inexplicable resistance t
their rational plans for exploiting the country. Continually the
were informed that their railways and factories could not take ce
tain routes or occupy certain positions The reasons given wer
impossible to understand, for they had no relevance, economic
social or political, to the problem of laying out an industrial ne
work. The Europeans were told that a certain range of hills was
terrestrial dragon and that no cutting could be made through it
tail. Tunnels through dragon hills were forbidden, and a propose
railway to run straight across low, flat country was rejected on th
grounds that the line would spoil the view from the hills. All thi
was laid down by practioners of the science of fung-shui, 'wind an
water', obscurely explained as 'that which can not be seen and ca
not be grasped.'

Below:

*Stonehenge on the Old
Sarum Ley Line.*

Endings

Beorh – *Anglo Saxon for a moated mound –'beorht' (adj.) = bright; burial mound or tumulus. It seems we get the ending -bury (unsurprisingly, referring to an earth covering) from this. (See also 'Burh'.)*

Black, Blake – *in Anglo-Saxon times meant shining, white, pale. Hence our words 'bleach', 'bleak'.*

Blackman or Coleman – *thus the minder of the fires at a beacon fire which is giving out light.*

Burh – *fortified or protected dwelling, hill top camps (e.g. Old Sarum) –it seems that we get the ending -bury (e.g. Salisbury) from this as well as from 'Beorh' (above).*

Cole, Coel, Cold – *Welsh: coel certh = 'omen of danger', beacon, bonfire ; (obsolete) juggler, wizard, diviner (a dowser even?) (Old King Cole?); a belief, an omen. The Coleman or Blackman – would then be revered figure, connected with religious significance and the maintenance of the beacon fire.*

Dod, Dood, Toot – *a rounded mound, or hill (e.g. Totnes, in Devon); also means a staff, club. Dodman – (perhaps also by misuse 'Deadman') a person using such tools. The implication being that a surveyor of a track would use them. Indeed surveyors today still do when siting from a theodolite.*

Garn – *Welsh for tumulus, or burial mound.*

Heol, heel – *road, way , track (Stonehenge has a Heel Stone – said to be because it has a footprint in it, more likely this is a modern or Christianised, sanitised version of the old Celtic word. Interestingly also, the classic picture of the sun rising over the Heel Stone is not necessarily correct (according to Christopher Chippendale, in* Stonehenge Complete, *1994). He maintains there is evidence that there were two Heel Stones which framed the rising summer solstice sun as it rose between them. If true, this makes the old Celtic word for road or path seem a very likely derivation, since the line of the sun would have come straight from the sun, through the gap (or gate) between the Heel Stones and into the circle.*

Ley – *in Anglo-Saxon meant clearing, glade, cultivated land, pasture, enclosed field. Root in 'lake' means reflection. (See also 'Leye' and 'Mote'.)*
Alternatives: lay, lei, ley, leigh, lea, lee,
Note: 'The lay of the land', 'the lie of the land' implication more of a survey than reference to a field.

Leye – *(obsolete) island, (obsolete) flame, bright.*

Mote – *speck of light, or something in the eye.*

Tan – *Celtic for 'fire' (has perhaps been Christianized as outside Salisbury where 'Tan Hill' has become 'St Anne's Hill').*

Toot – *see **Dod**. Also the 'Tutti-Man' of Hungerford, N. Wiltshire, still parades the town once a year, carrying a six foot long staff – a remnant of his occupation(?).*

Tump – *hill.*

Useful OLD ENGLISH WORDS

Bibliography

Bord, Janet & Colin, *Mysterious Britain*, 1974, Granada Publishing; *The Secret Country*, 1978 Paladin.

Burl, Aubrey *Prehistoric Avebury*, 1979, Yale University.

Chippindale, Christopher, *Stonehenge Complete*, 1994, Thames & Hudson.

Dames, Michael, *The Silbury Treasure*, 1992, Thames & Hudson; *The Avebury Cycle*, 1996, Thames & Hudson.

Dartnell & Goddard, *Wiltshire Words*, 1894, Wiltshire Life Society.

Devereux, Paul *The New Ley Hunter's Guide*, 1994, Gothic Image Publications; *The Old Straight Tracks of Wessex*, 1992, Thornhill Press.

Harte, Jeremy, *Cuckoo Pounds and Singing Barrows*, 1986, Dorset Archaeological Society.

Hitching, Francis, *Earth Magic*, 1976, London.

Michell, John *The View Over Atlantis*, 1969, Garnstone Press Ltd.

Stackhouse, Thomas, *Illustration of the Tumuli*, 1806.

Thom, A. *Megalithic Sites in Britain*, 1967, Oxford Press.

Underwood, Guy, *Patterns of the Past*, 1970, Pitman.

Watkins, Alfred, *The Old Straight Track* (1925 Methuen & Co.) 1970 Garnstone Press; *The Ley Hunter's Guide*, 1927 & 1983, Turnstone Press.

Watson, Lyall, *Supernature*, 1973, Hodder & Stoughton.

Whitlock, Ralph, *Water Divining & Other Dowsing – A Practical Guide*, 1982 Hale.

Wilson, Colin, *Starseekers*, 1980, Hodder & Stoughton.

Acknowledgements

For the use of illustrations and photographs the publishers gratefully thank:

Aerofilms, pp. 11, 12, 15;
John Crook, pp. 2, 18, 19, 23, 26;
Alexander Grenfell, pp. 16, 21 top;
Jürgen Krönig, pp. 3, 21 bottom, 24;
Michael Mathias, pp. 8;
Simon McBride, p. 28;
Ralph Whitlock, p. 17;

Line drawings (pp. 6, 7) by John Fuller.

Cover illustrations by Matthew Harvey.

All design, computer graphics and computer typesetting produced by Alexander S. Grenfell.

Published by Wessex Books 1998, reprinted 2003, 2004. Revised edition 2008, Reprinted 2012

Text © Roger Crisp.

Design © Wessex Books 2008.

Printed in India.

ISBN 978-0-9529619-3-2